ANIMALS
IN HOT AND COLD PLACES

MALCOLM PENNY

Wayland

HOT AND COLD PLACES

TITLES IN THIS SERIES

Animals in Hot and Cold Places
Clothes in Hot and Cold Places
Food and Farming in Hot and Cold Places
Homes in Hot and Cold Places

Series editor: Geraldine Purcell
Series designer: Helen White

Cover: (left) Lions living on the grasslands of Africa have to cope with incredible heat – even during the wet season. (right) This polar bear spends the winter months hunting on the sea ice of the Arctic region.

Title page: The mottled-brown colouring of the hyena's fur helps it to blend in with the dry grasses of the African plains.

© Copyright 1994 Wayland (Publishers) Limited

First published in 1994 by Wayland (Publishers) Limited
61 Western Road, Hove, East Sussex BN3 1JD, England

British Library Cataloguing in Publication Data
Penny, Malcolm
 Animals in Hot and Cold Places. – (Hot & Cold Places Series)
  I. Title II. Price, David III. Series 591

ISBN 0 7502 0809 0

Typeset by White Design
Printed and bound in Great Britain by BPC Paulton Books Ltd., Paulton

CONTENTS

TOO HOT OR TOO COLD?	4
LIFE AT THE POLES	6
KEEPING WARM IN COLD CLIMATES	10
KEEPING COOL IN HOT PLACES	12
DESERT DWELLERS	14
THE POLAR BEAR'S YEAR	16
LIONS: HUNTING IN THE WET AND DRY	18
NIGHT AND DAY ON THE PLAINS	20
ANIMALS ON THE MOVE	22
A CORAL REEF	24
WONDERS UNDER THE ICE	26
THE HUMAN FACTOR	28
GLOSSARY	30
FURTHER READING	31
INDEX	32

TOO HOT OR TOO COLD?

There are very few places where it is too hot or too cold for animals to live. For example, the crater of an active volcano would be much too hot and the areas around the North and South Poles, which are freezing all year round, are too cold.

All animals need a good supply of food and fresh water to survive. They also need suitable places to breed and raise their young.

There is a wide variety of animals living in the seas and on land which survive in very different climates. The bodies and behaviour of animals in different climatic regions have adapted (changed) over millions of years to suit their climate and the seasonal changes.

This is especially true for animals living in the Arctic or Antarctic regions. They breed and raise their young during the few milder summer months before the icy winter sets in again.

▼ These tube worms live in very high temperatures around hot-water springs on the bed of the Pacific Ocean. The tube worms can be as big as three metres long.

A HOT HOME

Deep beneath the surface of the oceans it is too dark and cold for plants to grow, so there is little animal life. One exception to this is a special type of tube worm which lives around hot-water springs on the sea-bed of the Pacific Ocean. The hot-water springs are formed by the great heat from inside the Earth being released through cracks in the Earth's crust and the sea-bed. These tube worms are the only animals that can live at such high temperatures – without plants or other animals to eat. They get their energy by using minerals and chemicals from the rocks in the sea-bed that the hot water has passed through.

A COLD HOME

No land animals live inside the Antarctic Circle. During winter the seas around the Antarctic continent freeze and the ice may extend as far as 2,800 kilometres around the South Pole. In midwinter, the temperature can be as low as -70°C.

The only land animals that can survive in these low temperatures are two types of mite and a type of springtail, which live on Signy Island, in the South Orkneys, just outside the Antarctic Circle. These animals are one or two millimetres long. In winter, when the island is covered in snow, the animals hibernate. The mites and the springtails have a special chemical in their bodies which stops them from freezing during winter. As the ice melts in the summer, they come out of hibernation and are active once more.

▼ Springtails live almost everywhere in the world, wherever they can find food and water.

LIFE AT THE POLES

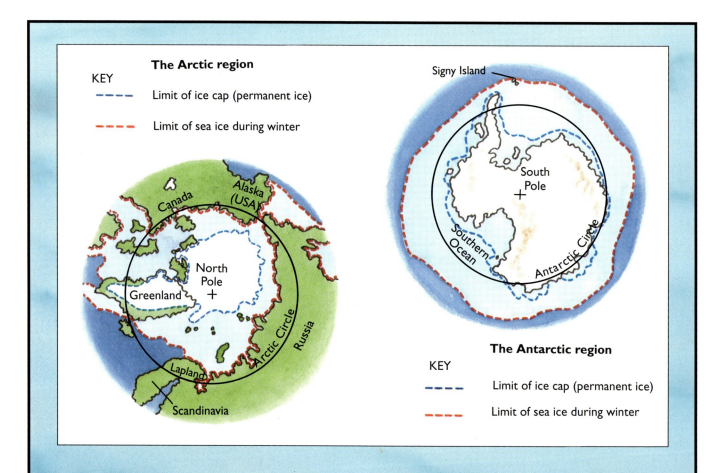

THE POLAR REGIONS

The Arctic and the Antarctic are very different, although they are both cold and covered in snow and ice.

Under the ice, the Arctic region is mostly sea around the North Pole. There are many islands and landmasses inside the Arctic Circle, including northern Russia, Canada, Scandinavia, Finland, Greenland and Alaska (USA). Animals cannot live all year round on the sea ice so they spend part of the year on these Arctic lands.

The Antarctic continent is land, covered in thick ice and surrounded by frozen sea most of the year. It is too cold and dry for animals to live on the land. Penguins and seals only come to shore to breed on the outer limits of the landmass and surrounding islands.

◀ A polar bear diving into the icy water. The bear's thick coat traps air near its skin to keep it warm. Polar bears live in the Arctic region.

▼ Penguins live in the Antarctic area. This Emperor penguin chick is only two weeks old.

The only animals that travel inland to breed on the Antarctic continent are the Emperor penguins and the Antarctic petrels. During summer 300,000 petrels flock to Scullin Monolith, one of the few rocky peaks that become free of ice, to lay their eggs and raise chicks.

Emperor penguins travel inland in autumn to breed. During the icy winter the males hold the single egg in a special pouch of skin to keep it warm with their body. The females return to the sea to hunt for food to bring back when the chicks have hatched.

▲ Polar bears eat whatever they can catch, although they prefer seals. This polar bear has caught an Eider duck. An adult polar bear is over three metres long and is a fierce hunter.

Both polar regions have a good supply of food in the sea. The main food is krill – tiny, shrimp-like animals. The blue whale is the largest animal ever to have lived on Earth. It lives in the polar seas and feeds on krill. Other polar animals rely on a good supply of krill in one way or another. Polar bears, for example, feed mainly on seals, but some of these seals eat krill and others eat fish which have fed on krill.

Among the krill-eaters in the Antarctic are several types of penguin, such as the Emperor and Chinstrap penguins. Penguins cannot fly but they are fast and graceful swimmers and are experts at catching fish. Penguins can live in the Antarctic because there are no predators on the land. In the Arctic, where polar bears and Arctic foxes are common, flightless birds would be easy prey when they came ashore to breed. The penguins' enemies in the Antarctic are in the sea. Leopard seals and killer whales hunt them as they leave the breeding beaches to feed.

▼ **A leopard seal has caught a young penguin. Leopard seals are ruthless hunters – they wait for the penguin chicks to make their first attempt to swim, and then strike!**

KEEPING WARM IN COLD CLIMATES

Animals that live in cold places keep warm by being well insulated. They may have a layer of fat, called blubber, or a thick hairy coat to keep in their body heat.

Animals that have blubber include whales, dolphins, seals and walruses. Seals and walruses, which must come ashore to breed, may be in danger of overheating while they are lying in the sunshine. When they are too hot, seals and walruses can lose heat through their blubber. Warm blood flows nearer the skin's surface so that the heat can escape quickly.

▲ **Walrus males basking in the sunshine on Round Island, off the coast of Alaska, USA. Walruses have a very thick layer of blubber to help to keep them warm in the icy polar waters.**

◀ **This polar bear is trapped on the land during the summer. It is waiting for the seas to freeze so that it can go hunting on the winter ice.**

FUR COATS

The hairy coat of polar bears and caribou (the North American name for reindeer) is a very good insulator. Their coats have a thick layer of underfur and the outer hairs are hollow and filled with air. Heat travels very slowly through the air-filled hairs so they trap the body heat for a longer time than normal animal fur.

◀ The caribou's thick fur coat keeps the animal warm even in freezing temperatures.

Penguins, like all birds, have two layers of feathers – fluffy down feathers next to the skin and an outer layer of smooth feathers. The down feathers trap warm air and the outer feathers stop the body heat from escaping. The outer feathers also make the penguins streamlined for swimming underwater.

▶ Penguins are well insulated by their layers of feathers. These are Chinstrap penguins, on Bird Island in the Antarctic.

KEEPING COOL

▶ Lionesses panting to keep cool in the hot African sun. They must drink water every day to make up for what they lose by panting.

Animals in hot places need to be able to lose heat rather than keep it in. Sweating and panting are both ways of losing heat, but they involve losing water as it dries from the skin or mouth. Panting and sweating are only useful if the animal can replace the water it has lost. Desert animals, such as the kangaroo rat from the deserts of Arizona, in the USA, cannot afford to lose water and so they do not pant or sweat.

IN HOT PLACES

Birds, such as snake birds in northern Australia, can lose heat by opening their beaks and fluttering the skin of their throats. This cools the blood at the skin's surface without losing any water. The snake bird also lifts its wings and ruffles its feathers to allow cool air next to the skin.

The ostrich is a good example of a tropical bird which has areas of bare skin without any feathers, to help the body lose heat.

Some animals can only survive in hot countries by wallowing in mud or water during the day. In Africa, hippopotamuses leave their wallows only at night to feed. Crocodiles and alligators keep near to rivers or water-holes so they can cool off in the water if they get too hot.

▲ A snake bird in Australia spreading its wings to cool off in the breeze.

◀ Water buffalo, in southeast Asia, keep cool by wallowing wherever they can find water or mud.

DESERT DWELLERS

▲ A dune lizard in the Namib Desert, Africa, lifting each foot in turn from the hot sand to cool in the air.

Desert animals have to cope not only with heat but also with shortages of water and food. Deserts are very dry areas which have less than ten centimetres of rain each year. Desert plants only bloom when the rains come, so the desert animals live most of the year in a world of bare rock or loose, shifting sand.

All reptiles are cold-blooded and need the heat of the sun to warm their bodies so that they can be active. But reptiles cannot control their body heat, so if they become too hot they must cool down as soon as possible or they will die. Sometimes the behaviour of desert reptiles, such as lizards and snakes, can look very odd, but they have very good reasons for acting as they do. For example, the dune lizard from the Namib Desert in southern Africa, often stops as it travels over hot sand and lifts each foot off the sand in turn. When the sand in the shadow of its body has cooled, the lizard lies down on its underside with all four legs, head and tail held up in the air.

Many desert snakes move in a special way over the loose sand. A desert viper holds its body in loops, clear of the hot sand, so that it only touches in two or three places at any one time. This way of moving is called 'sidewinding'.

WATER SAVERS

The darkling beetle, from the Namib Desert, collects water at dawn by standing with its tail in the air. As the moisture in the early morning air condenses (forms as water droplets) on the beetle's body, the drops run down its back and into its mouth.

Most desert animals get the water they need from their food. A kangaroo rat stores dry seeds and berries near the entrance to its burrow. As the animal sleeps, the moisture from its breath forms as water on the food store. When the kangaroo rat wakes up, it eats the seeds and berries straight away and takes in the water it lost while it slept.

▲ **A darkling beetle drinking droplets of water formed from the morning mist.**

◄ **A desert viper sidewinding in the Namib Desert. This is a good way for the viper to move quickly and to keep its body away from the hot sand.**

THE POLAR BEAR'S YEAR

The Arctic winter lasts from September to April or May. Even in the summer months the temperature around the Arctic Circle rarely goes above 10°C. But this is enough to encourage the plants to bloom on the tundra, the region at the edge of the Arctic Circle, and for seals and walruses to come ashore to breed.

With such a great food supply around, this is the time to see female polar bears with cubs. The female polar bear spends the whole winter in a den with her cubs. The cubs are born in midwinter and weigh about 650 grammes, but by the time they leave the den in March they weigh 10 kilogrammes and are the size of small dogs.

During the summer, a female leads her cubs across the ice. She catches young seals for them to eat and teaches them how to find food for themselves. Polar bears raid the nests of birds and eat the eggs and young chicks. The female polar bear continues to give her cubs milk until they are two years old. By autumn the female and her cubs must be as fat as possible because they will soon be going back to a den to hibernate during the winter. They will not have anything to eat until the following spring.

Female polar bears with cubs are the only ones to spend the whole winter in a den. Other adults roam the ice around the southern edge of the Arctic and

▲ **A polar bear eating the skin and blubber of a fat young seal.**

▶ **A female polar bear leads her two one-year-old cubs in search of food in the snowy Arctic spring.**

hunt for seals. Seals can stay underwater for long periods of time as they fish under the ice. But they need to breathe air and must use a hole in the ice to reach the surface. Polar bears hunt seals by creeping up on them as the seals lie next to their breathing-holes or poke their heads above the water. The polar bear usually eats only the seal's blubber, which is a good source of energy.

LIONS: HUNTING

Lions do not have to change their behaviour to survive a cold season – it is always hot on the grassland plains of Africa. But the climate is divided between a dry season and a wet season – often called 'the rains'.

Lions live in groups called prides. A pride contains between four and twelve adult females and their cubs, with two or three males to guard the pride's territory. The whole pride moves about together in search of good hunting grounds.

In the dry season, hunting is easy. The lions stay near a water-hole and wait for their prey to come to drink. When the prey, such as a zebra, finally lowers its head to drink, the lionesses pounce. It is usually the females who hunt and catch food for the pride. During the dry season the lions hunt by day.

When the rains come the grass grows and the African plains turn green. Herds of grazing animals,

▲ A lioness with two well-grown cubs sitting by a water-hole during the dry season.

IN THE WET AND DRY

▶ A pride of lions feasting on a buffalo. There is plenty of food for all – even for the cubs.

▼ Lionesses do most of the hunting to support their pride. Here, a lioness is chasing a zebra across the plains.

such as zebra and wildebeest, can spread out and do not need to gather around water-holes. This makes it much more difficult for the lions to surprise their prey, so they begin to hunt at night. The females take the lead, spreading out in a line as they approach a herd. A young or weak-looking member of the herd is singled out and the lionesses close in for the kill. The pride shares the meal. The males are first to feast and then the lionesses. The cubs are always last, so that if there is not enough food for all the pride, the cubs will be the first to starve to death.

After a large meal the lions rest in a shady place – sometimes for days – until they have digested their food. Then the hunting starts again.

NIGHT AND DAY ON THE PLAINS

▼ **(MAIN PICTURE)** Zebra can find plenty of food on the grassy plains of Africa. Also, there are few trees to give predators cover.
▼ **(INSET)** A hyena prowling through the bush, on the lookout to steal another predator's prey.

Although it can be very hot, life on the grassland plains of Africa is not so hard as in the deserts. As long as there has been a good rainy season there is usually enough food for the plant-eating animals, such as zebra and giraffe. Tropical plains support so many different animals that they are divided into two groups. Some are active in the daytime and others come out at night – these are called nocturnal animals.

At night, leopards come down from the trees where they have been resting and hyenas come out of their dens. Leopards usually hunt antelope. The leopard takes a resting herd by surprise under the cover of darkness and carries off its prey. A leopard must drag its meal up a tree quickly if it is to avoid a pack of hyenas stealing it away. A leopard will not fight to keep its meal because it cannot afford to be injured and unable to hunt.

▶ **Leopards hunt at night. They take their prey up a tree, to stop hyenas from stealing it.**

ANIMALS ON THE MOVE

▲ **Wildebeest (gnus) move in huge herds across the grassy African plains. This herd is on the great plain of the Masai Mara, in Kenya.**

When animals move a long way in search of better conditions it is called migration. In southern Africa, wildebeest migrate across dry plains to places where it is raining. In Sudan, the white-eared kob migrates for the same reason. In northern Alaska, caribou travel south when winter comes and then move north again to have their young in the short Arctic summer.

Some of the longest migrations are made by birds. One, the Arctic tern, lives its life in permanent summer: it flies from north to south, following the sun, over the Atlantic Ocean. It breeds in the Arctic but travels south to feed during the northern winter.

The reason for travelling to the Arctic from warmer places to breed is that there are fewer animals in the north to compete with the migrating animals for food – or to hunt them as prey.

▲ Caribou have to cross many large rivers as they move between their breeding grounds in the north and their winter feeding areas to the south.

◀ An Arctic tern perched on an ice floe (a sheet of ice floating in the sea) near the coast of Canada. Soon it will migrate far to the south to find warmer weather.

A CORAL REEF

▶ Some coral polyps, such as these daisy corals, do not form reefs.

Near tropical shores, where the sea is shallow and clear, coral reefs grow. Coral looks like stone, but it is built by tiny animals called coral polyps. A polyp has a tube-shaped body with long, waving tentacles at the top. Polyps live together in large groups. Each one collects a mineral, called lime, from the water and uses it to build a tube around itself. A lot of these tubes joined together form a coral head and many coral heads together form a reef.

The polyps feed at night, catching prey from the water with their tentacles. The tentacles are covered in stinging cells. Once stung, the prey cannot move. Coral polyps eat the tiny swimming animals that are most common in shallow water at night.

Coral polyps can live only where sunlight can reach through the water. Each polyp has many tiny plant cells living inside it. These cells collect a chemical called carbon dioxide from inside the polyp and use the energy from sunlight to turn it into food. The plant cell benefits by being sheltered inside the polyp and the polyp gets a share of the food the plant produces.

Many other animals live on coral reefs. Shellfish and sea slugs creep over the surface, and hundreds of different small fish feed among the coral. Most of the fish are brightly coloured, so that they can recognize their own kind in the crowd. Larger fish prey on the small ones. Parrot fish eat the coral itself. They have pointed jaws, like a parrot's beak, with which they crunch up the hard, stony tubes.

▼ A shoal of yellow fin goatfish around the Great Barrier Reef, Australia. Tropical coral reefs are home to large numbers of small fish. The warm shallow waters around reefs provide plenty of food for all the animals that live there.

◄ A parrot fish crunching at a coral head with its strong beak-like mouth.

WONDERS UNDER THE ICE

▲ Under the Antarctic ice, the animals are as colourful as on a tropical reef. Sponges, anemones and starfish gather in the shelter of the rocks.

▼ Two humpback whales feeding on krill in the Arctic Ocean.

Under the frozen sea, close to shore, the Antarctic has as much colour and variety as a tropical coral reef. Giant sea anemones, colourful starfish and sponges live on the sea-bed and around the rocks. Limpets and sea urchins live among the dark-brown kelp (seaweed). On the sea-bed live huge sea spiders with ten legs, and giant sea lice, as big as grapefruit.

Further north, in the open water of the Antarctic, there is a problem. We already know about krill. It is the main food of whales, such as the blue and the humpback whales. The krill also feeds millions of penguins as well as fur seals, crabeater seals and many sea birds. Although there is a lot of krill in the polar oceans, there is not an unlimited supply.

The first explorers to sail in Antarctic waters said that there were so many whales that it was hard to avoid bumping into them. When whales were over-hunted, in the nineteenth and early twentieth centuries, many species became rare.

This meant that there was suddenly plenty of food available for all the other animals that eat krill. The better food supply increased the population of these animals, such as penguins and seals.

Now that whales are protected against being over-hunted, their numbers are beginning to rise again, but only very slowly. One reason for this is that they are now so rare that they hardly ever meet to breed. But the other reason is that their share of the krill is now being eaten by other animals. No one can tell whether the krill-eating whales will be able to get their food supply back, or whether the populations of seals and penguins will stay at their present level, leaving the whales to go hungry.

▼ Emperor penguins gather on the sea ice at Halley Bay. The cliff behind them is the edge of the Antarctic ice shelf.

THE HUMAN FACTOR

▲ Gentoo penguins nest beside the remains of an old British base which was used by explorers and scientists. It is forbidden to leave rubbish like this in the Antarctic now because it may damage the wildlife.

Hot and cold places, like other places, feel the harmful effects of human activities, such as industry and farming. The Antarctic should be the region which is least affected by human actions. The cold climate and its distance from other continents mean that very few people have ever been there. In the early 1990s, there were discussions about whether to protect the whole area from mining or oil-drilling.

People have lived in the Arctic region for thousands of years. For example, many Inuit now live in towns, but in the past they hunted polar bears and seals for food and lived in temporary homes on the ice.

The Inuit have always been careful not to harm their surroundings and to kill only what they can use.

The Arctic should be safe from becoming overpopulated because people find it hard to live there during the cold winters. But oil produced in Alaska, USA, has already caused some very bad pollution. Also, more and more people go there to hunt for sport. The presence of people and their machines is bound to cause damage to the region itself and the animals that live there.

There are more serious problems in the tropical areas. In many countries there are simply too many people. Every new mouth to feed means that more land must be used for farming. This in turn means that the animals will no longer be free to roam in search of food and water. The great rainforests are being chopped down, leaving many animals homeless. Even coral reefs will be affected as the shores become covered with villages and roads.

◀ The homes of many animals living in rainforests, such as this jaguar in Belize, Central America, are in danger of being destroyed if their surroundings are used for farming.

GLOSSARY

Antarctic The ice-covered continent around the South Pole. The Southern Ocean and the southern areas of the Indian, Atlantic and Pacific oceans freeze over in winter.

Antarctic Circle An imaginary circle around the world, 66°32' south of the equator. The Antarctic region is inside or close to this circle.

Arctic The area of frozen sea and ice-covered lands and islands around the North Pole.

Arctic Circle An imaginary circle around the world, 66°32' north of the equator. The Arctic region is inside or close to this circle.

breed When a male and a female animal produce young.

continent One of the Earth's seven large landmasses: Asia, Australia, Africa, Europe, North and South America and Antarctica are the continents.

cubs The name for the young of some animals, such as polar bears and seals.

digested When food has been broken down by chemicals inside the stomach so that it can be used for energy for the body.

hibernate To pass the winter in a sleep-like, inactive state. The animal only becomes active again when the weather becomes warmer.

insulated Covered with layers of fat, fur or material to stop heat from escaping.

landmasses Large, unbroken areas of land, such as continents.

Poles The ice-covered regions at the most northerly and southerly points of the Earth.

pollution Dirt, waste or chemicals in the environment (surroundings) which can be harmful to living things.
predators Animals that hunt and kill other animals for food.
prey Animals that are hunted and killed by other animals.
reptiles Cold-blooded animals with tough, scaly skin.
streamlined To be shaped with a smooth outline so that it is easy to travel through air or water.
territory The hunting or living area of an animal or family group of animals.
tropical To do with the hot areas of the world that lie between two imaginary lines around the Earth we call the Tropic of Cancer and the Tropic of Capricorn.
tundra The treeless plains of Arctic Europe, Asia and North America.

FURTHER READING

Jungle Animals edited by Mike Halson (Kingfisher Books, 1990)
The Penguin by Mike Linley (Boxtree, 1991)
The Lion by Caroline Brett (Boxtree, 1990)
What's Inside Sea Creatures? by Alexandra Parsons (Dorling Kindersley, 1993)

PICTURE ACKNOWLEDGEMENTS

Bruce Coleman Ltd. 18-19 (G. Ziesler); Eye Ubiquitous 11 (top) (G. R. Richardson); Images of Africa/D.K. Jones 19 (top), 29; F.L.P.A. 13 (bottom) (T. Whittaker); Institute of Oceanographic Scientists 4 (Woods Hole Institute); N.H.P.A. 7 (top) (B & C Alexander), 8 (B & C Alexander), 14-15 (A. Bannister), 15 (top) (A. Bannister), 16-17 (B & C Alexander), 20-21 (J. B. Blossom), *title page* & 21 (top) (A. Bannister), 26 (bottom) (R. Tidman); Oxford Scientific Films Ltd. *cover* (D. Cox), 9 (D. Allan), 10 (bottom) (D. Cox), 13 (top) (B. Wright), 14 (M. Fogden), 20 (inset) (R. Ben-Shahar), 25 (top) (F Bavendam), 25 (bottom) (J. Dorsey), 28 (D. Allan); Tony Stone Worldwide *cover* and 12 (N. Parfitt), 18 (top) (P. Lamberti), 22 (G. Kohler), 23 (bottom) (D. Hosking), 24 (D. Torckler); Survival Anglia Ltd. 5 (J. Foott), 7 (bottom) (M. Tracey), 10 (top) (J. Bennett), 11 (J. Bennett), 17 (J. Foott), 23 (top) (J. Bennett), 26 (top) (R. Price), 27 (M. Tracey). Inside artwork by David Price. Cover artwork by William Donohoe.

INDEX

Numbers in **bold** indicate entries which are illustrated.

Africa 12, 13, 14, 15, 18, 20, 22, 29
   dry season 18
   plains of **20-21**, 29
   wet season 18
Alaska (USA) 6, 22, 29
Antarctic 4, 5, **6-9**, 30
Arctic 4, **6-9**, 16, 17, 23, 30
Arctic foxes 9
Arctic terns 23
Atlantic Ocean 23
Australia 13, 25

Belize, Central America 29
blubber 10, 17
breeding 4, 6, 9, 10, 16, 30

Canada 6
caribou (see reindeer)
climates 4, 18
coral polyps **24**, 25
coral reefs 24, **25**, 29

desert animals 12, 14-15
   darkling beetles **15**
   kangaroo rats 15
dolphins 10

Finland 6

giraffe 20
Greenland 6

hibernation 5, 16, 30
hippopotamuses 13
hunting 17, **18-19**, 21, 23
hyenas 20

Inuit 28-29

jaguar **29**

keeping cool 12-13
   wallows 13
keeping warm 10-11
   blubber 10, 17
   fur coats **11**
krill 8, 26, 27

leopards 20, **21**
lions **12**, **18-19**

migration 22-3
mites 5

Namib Desert, Africa 14, 15
nocturnal animals 21

ostriches 13

Pacific Ocean 4
parrot fish **25**
penguins 6, **7**, 9, **11**, **27**, **28**
   Chinstrap 9, **11**
   Emperor **7**, 9, **27**
   Gentoo **28**
petrels 7
polar bears **7**, **8**, **10**, **11**, **16-17**
pollution 29, 30

rainforests 29
reindeer **11**, **22-23**
reptiles 13, **14**, **15**, 30
   alligators 13
   crocodiles 13
   dune lizards **14**
   snakes **14-15**
Russia 6

Scandinavia 6
sea anemones **26**
seals 8, **9**, 10, 16, 17, 26, 27
   leopard seal **9**
Signy Island 5, 6
snake bird **13**
southeast Asia 13
sponges **26**
springtails **5**
starfish **26**

tube worms **4**
tundra 16

walruses **10**, 16
waterbuffalo **13**
water-holes **13**, 18
whales 8, 9, **26**
   blue whales 8, 26
   humpback whales **26**
   killer whales 9
wildebeest 18, 22

zebra 18, 19, **20-21**